TAKE HEART

TAKE HEART

The Ways of Love, Free of Fear and Ego

David Richo

2024 Revised Edition

Table of Contents

Introduction

Over the years readers have especially appreciated certain passages and practices in my books. I have gathered and revised them and now share them with you in what follows.

I have learned from many spiritual traditions, from many people, and from my own experience. I have been blessed to discover something of what it means to live in upright ways, show loving-kindness toward ourselves and others, and free ourselves from ego and fear. This book offers insights and practices that can help us live our lives at those psychologically healthy and spiritually conscious levels.

Our thrilling human destiny is to display in our lifetime the timeless design of love and wholeness that has always been inside us. Choices and attitudes that show integrity and loving-kindness help that happen.

Yes, we can take heart, that is, grow in hope and courage no matter how chaotic the world becomes or how disappointing people may be to us.

Then we joyously see our self-esteem and our spirituality flourish. They are the true paths to contentment with ourselves as we are and can be and with the world as it is and may be. All it takes is heart.

There will never be only love or only peace
but there can be more love
than before we got here
and more peace
because we stayed here in peace and with love.

Something,
We know not what,
Is always and everywhere
lovingly at work,
we know not how,
to make the world more than it is now
to make us more than we are yet.
That Something is what we call:
a Higher Power,
the life force of the universe,
our own true nature,
one Sacred Heart of love, never apart.

From: *How to be an Adult in Love* (Shambhala)

What Makes Us Human

Every human comes into the world equipped with wonderful gifts. They form our collective human inheritance, resources in all of us, qualities that make us truly human:

Our ability to go on loving no matter how we are treated by others and no matter what happened to us in the past

Our ability to say no to abuse and not to engage in it ourselves

Our outrage at and courageous action in the face of evil

Our willingness to put ourselves second, even to risk our life for others

Our capacity to forgive and let go

Our grief at the loss of those we love

Our refusal, at times, to accept defeat no matter what the odds

Our yes to acceptance of defeat, when the evidence demands it

Our irrepressible playfulness and sense of humor

Our unflappable hope

Our longings for love, meaning, freedom, happiness, and growth no matter how many times we fail to find them

Our knack for showing our best when things are at their worst

Our skill at finding order in chaos and meaning in disaster

Our intuition, which reveals more than we logically know

Our commitment to acting honestly and unselfishly even when no one is looking

Our striving for what lies beyond our grasp, our inclination to stretch ourselves

Our power to say, do, or be what leads to healing ourselves and others

We have it in us to find an opportunity for growth in all that happens

Our trust that evil is never the last word, that love is the strongest force on earth

Our ability to say yes unconditionally to the givens of life, implacable though they be

Our kindly understanding of and loving reaching out to those who do not choose to live in accord with this list

These ineffaceable graces show us why we never give up on ourselves or others. They are also the firm basis of our trust in ourselves, in the human community, and in a higher power.

From: *How to Be an Adult in Faith and Spirituality* (Paulist Press, 2011)

There are certain facts we cannot change, unavoidable "givens" of human life and of relationships:

1) Everything changes and ends

2) Things do not always go according to plan

3) Life is not always fair

4) Pain is part of life

5) People are not loving and loyal all the time

It is hard to find serenity in life until we acknowledge and come to terms with these facts. This means giving up trying to control them. Instead, we witness them mindfully, that is without judgment or complaint. We let ourselves feel grief for each of them and for how they have impacted us personally, familially, relationally, and societally.

We cultivate an "unconditional yes" to these conditions of existence. We learn to open, accept, even embrace our predicaments without trying to control their outcomes. These five givens are the ingredients for our evolving in character, depth, and compassion. Spiritually we begin to trust what happens as opportunities to practice mindfulness and loving-kindness.

Once we begin to do that, we come to realize that these givens actually offer us profound opportunities for growth. Then a new honesty and realism begins to take shape in us.

Here are affirmations that help us say yes without protest or complaint:

More and more, I have the serenity to accept the things I cannot change.

More and more, I have the courage to change the things I can change.

I am open to the grace that shows me the difference.

"I say Yes to the past as it was. I say Yes to the present as it is. I say Yes to the future as it shall turn out to be."

My Yes to what is and to how I and others are is unconditional.

Now I trust that everything that happens to me is somehow a grace, a light that will not go out, something enfolding me and unfolding in me.

From: *Five True Things: A Little Guide to Embracing Life's Big Challenges* (Shambhala, 2019)

In the face of life's implacable givens, we might take refuge in superstitious thoughts or magical rituals of safety we devise to protect ourselves from what we fearfully believe is a scary, unpredictable, and dangerous world. This is magical thinking, using our wishes or fears to explain what is happening or can happen or to find a way to protect ourselves from peril. We try to control the uncontrollable. We try to explain the unexplainable. We try to console ourselves with illusions. Here are some examples of magical thinking:

» Reality will become or remain the same as my mental picture of it.

» Dangerous forces will erupt if I do not adhere to very precise rules or rituals.

» Happiness is a reward for being good; pain is a punishment for being bad.

» I have to grasp this opportunity right now or lose it. There is no time for a mindful pause.

» Need fulfillment and love is scarce, so I must work hard and consider myself lucky to deserve it.

» If people knew me as I really am, they would not love me or want me.

» "What goes around, comes around." This is a wish of the frustrated retaliatory ego, rather than a karmic certainty.

» If I do not remain in control, everything will fall apart.

» If I bring a problem out into the open, it will become even more serious and dangerous. If I never mention it, it will go away.

» If something is good it won't last; if it is bad it will get worse.

» If I love something I will lose it or have it taken away from me.

» Happiness will not last if I enjoy it too much. Full-on exuberance is dangerous.

» If it had not been for this one thing happening or if one special thing would happen, everything would be perfect now.

» Prosperity will be followed by catastrophe: "A bull market has a bear behind it" and vice versa.

» There is a by-and-by to come when there will be no violence or evil and the human shadow will disappear.

From: *When Catholic Means Cosmic: Opening to a Big-Hearted Faith* (Paulist Press, 2015)

Affirmations to Free Ourselves
from the Grip of Fear

I trust my appropriate fears to give me signals of real danger.

I see that I also have unreal fears and worries.

More and more I recognize the difference between real and imagined fears.

I feel compassion toward myself for all the years I have been afraid.

I forgive those who hypnotized me into unreal fears.

I trust that I have as much fearlessness in me as fear.

I trust the strength that opens in me when I have to face something.

I believe in myself as able to handle what comes my way today.

I create a pause between a trigger and my response.

I have the inner resources to handle any fear or trigger.

I find support inside and outside myself.

I have an enormous capacity for re-building, restoring, and recovering from fear.

I am more and more sure of my abilities.

I am more and more aware of how I hold fear in my body.

I relax the part of my body that holds my fear.

I am freeing my body from the grip of fear.

I open my body to joy and serenity.

I let go of the stress and tension that come from fear.

I let go of my fears of sickness, accident, old age, and death.

I let go of my fear of the future.

I let go of regretful ties to the past.

I let go of any tie I may still have to judgments my parents had of me.

I let go of my fear of the unknown.

I cease being afraid of knowing, having, or showing my feelings.

I am less and less scared by what happens, by what has happened, by what will happen.

I let go of my fear of what might happen.

I let go of my obsessive thoughts about how the worst will happen.

I let go of fear-based thoughts.

I trust myself always to find a solution.

I catch myself when I engage in paranoid fantasies and I let them go.

My trust in myself is releasing me from fear and fearsome fantasies.

I let go of regretting my mistakes; I find the path to going on.

I let go of basing my decisions on fear.

I let go of finding something to fear in everything.

I let go of believing that everything is dangerous and headed for disaster.

I see the humor in my exaggerated reactions to unreal dangers.

I find a humorous response to every irrational fear.

I smile at my scared ego and shrug off its relationship fears:

I let go of my fear of aloneness or of time on my hands.

I let go of my fear of abandonment.

I let go of my fear of closeness.

I let go of my fear of commitment.

I let go of my fear of being vulnerable.

I let go of my fear of giving or receiving.

I let go of my fear of loving or being loved.

I let go of believing I have to measure up to what others want me to be.

I give up having to be perfect.

I let go of my performance fears.

I let go of my sexual fears.

I am confident in my ability to deal with people or situations that scare me.

I let go of my fear of any person.

I let go of my fear of saying No to others.

I let go of my fear of saying Yes.

I cease being intimidated by others' anger.

I give up trying to appease those who intimidate me.

Attempts to bully me now fall flat.

I let go of being on the defensive.

I protect myself while always being committed to non-violence.

I stick to my guns and I hold my fire.

I let go of feeling obliged to do things his/her/their way.

I let go of the need to meet others' expectations.

I state and protect my personal boundaries.

I let go of my fear of what might happen if people dislike me.

I let go of my terror about disapproval, ridicule, exclusion, or rejection.

I dare to stop auditioning for people's approval or love.

I give up the need to correct people's impressions of me.

I give up my poses, pretenses, and posturings; I dare to be myself.

I dare to show my hand, to show my passions, to show my enthusiasms, to show my real feelings, longings, and needs.

I want my every word, feeling, and deed to reveal me as I truly am.

I give up being afraid of what I want.

I ask for what I want.

I love being found out, caught in the act of being my authentic self.

I dare to live the life that truly reflects my deepest needs and wishes.

I let go of the fear that I will lose, lose money, lose face, lose freedom, lose friends, lose family members, lose respect, lose status, lose my job, lose out.

I let go of my fear of spending, saving, and sharing money.

I let go of my fear of having to grieve.

I let go of fears about my adequacy as a parent or child, partner or friend.

I let go of my fear of the fearsome givens of life: impermanence, change, suffering, unfairness, failed plans, losses, and betrayals.

I am flexible enough to accept life as it is.

I am forgiving enough to accept how I have lived my life so far.

I trust my present predicament as a path.

I let go of control; I let the chips fall where they may.

I let go of more than any fate can take away from me.

I cease being afraid of my own power.

I cease being afraid of the power of others.

I let go of my fear of authority.

I speak truth to power.

I dare to take a stand for the oppressed and the marginalized.

I join with the most vulnerable in our society.

I dare to devote my life to co-creating a world of justice, peace, and love.

As I show courage for social justice, I notice I am letting go of fear in all areas of my life.

I trust ever-renewing sources of bravery within me.

I let go of having any fear stop or drive me.

Nothing forces me; nothing holds me back.

I am a hero: I live through pain and am transformed by it.

I show grace under pressure.

I stop running; I stop hiding.

I have pluck and wit.

I meet danger face to face.

I stand up to a fight.

I speak up for myself.

I speak up for others.

I let go of hesitation and self-doubt.

I notice primitive dreads in me, for example:

If I love something I will lose it or have it taken away from me.

If something is good it won't last.

What is bad will get worse.

I recognize these beliefs as superstitions and let go of the fears that support them.

I take risks and yet I act with responsibility and caring.

I keep finding alternatives behind the apparent dead-end of fear.

I let go of scanning my life to find a reason to be afraid.

More and more my fear is becoming healthy excitement.

I let fear go and let joy in.

I let fear go and let love in.

I am grateful for the love that awaits me everywhere.

I know I am deeply loved by many people near and far.

I feel lovingly held by a higher power (God, Universe, Buddha, etc.).

As I devote myself more and more to a higher power than myself I feel it alive through, with, and in me.

I believe that I have an important destiny and that I am living in accord with it.

I am more and more aware of others' fears, more and more sensitive to them, more and more compassionate toward them.

I enlarge my circle of love to include every living being.

I keep finding ways to show my love.

I am great-hearted and bold-spirited.

I let go of ill-will toward those who have hurt me.

I do good to those who hate me, bless those who curse me, pray or wish enlightenment to those who have mistreated me.

I can say "Ouch!" and open a dialogue rather than retaliate.

I dare to give of myself unconditionally and I dare to be unconditionally committed to maintaining my own boundaries.

I honor and evoke my animal powers, my human powers, my divine powers.

I set free my love, till now imprisoned by fear.

I set free my joy, till now inhibited by fear.

I let true love cast out fear.

May I always choose the path of gentle love, the best antidote to fear.

I say yes to all that happens to me today as an opportunity to love more and fear less.

I keep letting go and I keep going on.

I feel an enduring fearlessness awakening in me.

I keep affirming my freedom from fear.

I am thankful for the grace of finding freedom from fear.

May all beings find freedom from fear.

The certainty that nothing can happen to us
that does not belong to us in our innermost being,
is the foundation of fearlessness....
Then life has lost its horrors
and suffering its sting.

–Lama Govinda: *Foundations of Tibetan Mysticism*

From: *When Love Meets Fear* (Paulist Press)

Some actions evoke a reaction simply because of an injustice toward us.

At other times, we might have a reaction that seems bigger than the event warrants or hangs on and eats away at us. Perhaps it is then pointing to something unnoticed in ourselves. We can do our best to **S.E.E.** what is going on:

Is this my **S**hadow? Our shadow is the part of ourselves that we do not notice but that we project onto others. It is our negative shadow if we see unacceptable or mean traits or behaviors in others and imagine they are not also possible—or even occasionally activated— in us. We can ask if what has upset us is something like our own hidden, disavowed, or unnoticed self and commit ourselves to acknowledge it. This is how we befriend our shadow side. *Clue: we might find ourselves strongly blaming the other.*

Is this my **E**go? Our ego can be so inflated that we are overly sensitive to others' reactions to us. We are aroused to fury or indignation when our greatness is not honored, when we are called on our shortcomings, when we are shown to be wrong, when we are not granted full control, or even when we are given well-meant feedback. Then we become defensive and want to lash out. We can notice those reactions and work with our wounded ego to calm down, accept our fallibility, and look for what we can learn about ourselves when we are not defensive. *Clue: we might want to retaliate, the ego's favorite sport.*

Is this an issue from my Earlier life? Our unfinished business from childhood, or past relationships, may come to the fore when someone reminds us of how we were treated in the past. The manner of an authority figure today may be reminiscent of how our parents acted toward us in childhood. The betrayal by someone today may remind us of how a former partner treated us. We react to a person or situation as if they were here and now but they are actually recreating the past in the present. The work is to acknowledge that transference and to break through it so we can stay present and stay in the present. *Clue: we might feel the powerlessness of childhood.*

We can use the SEE acronym when we are upset by asking ourselves:

Is this my own shadow I am looking at?

Is this my ego feeling indignant?

Is this reminding me of my childhood?

From: *When the Past Is Present: Healing the Emotional Wounds That Sabotage Our Relationships* (Shambhala, 2008)

18

The five *A*s, our original needs: attention, affection, appreciation, acceptance, allowing foster secure attachment—both in our childhood and in our adult relationships. Fortunately, as children all it takes for safety and security to happen is to have our needs satisfied with good enough parenting. We do not need perfection, nor is it possible.

The following ideals apply either to one or both of your parents:

Attention:

You felt that your parents, or at least one of them, directed an engaged focus on you.

You felt they were paying mindful attention to you with no judgment or reproach of you.

They looked not at you but into you to know your feelings and needs.

They asked you what you felt and needed without trying to convince you otherwise.

They attuned to your feelings and needs in a mirroring way.

They checked in with you about your reactions to them and to family events.

You knew you would be heard, that your story and emotions were of genuine interest to them and gained a welcoming response.

They loved knowing you.

Affection:

Your parents hugged, held, and kissed you.

They showed their love in physical ways without being inappropriate.

You often heard them tell you that they loved you.

No one was embarrassed by eye contact or touch.

You felt that your experience was cradled with benevolent fondness ever-expanding.

You knew without a doubt that your parents' caring connection to you would never end.

They welcomed affection from you in your way of showing it.

Their ways of showing love evolved in accord with your age but never lessened.

You know they had wanted you even before you were born and that they always will.

You felt you were irreplaceable.

Appreciation:

You were valued by your parents for yourself not for your accomplishments.

You did not feel that you were a burden or "another mouth to feed."

Your parents did not play favorites.

They appreciated your uniquely important place in their lives and in that of the whole family.

They acknowledged your gifts, gave you credit for them, did what they could to boost them.

Your parents backed you up if and when others turned against you.

They understood your joys and tears and held them in an equally warm embrace.

You knew you could always trust them.

Acceptance:

You knew that whatever you were or would turn out to be was acceptable to them.

You knew they were not trying to make you into what they wanted you to be but curious about what you yourself would grow into.

They showed you that your interests were totally acceptable to them.

They accepted your feelings, needs, lifestyle.

They accepted your sexual and gender orientation with no reprimand or suggestion you be otherwise than what you were.

All your feelings were OK, rather than some being judged as wrong, e.g., "Boys don't cry."

You were not shamed.

You did not have to try to fit in to the family; you always knew you belonged.

Allowing:

Your parents tried their best to know your deepest needs, values, and wishes.

They were not insisting that these needs, values, and wishes had to mirror their own.

They were not trying to control you but they did set reasonable limits to guide you.

You felt free to explore the world around you rather than being held back or obliged to care-take them.

They loved having you find new ways of thinking and imagining even when your ways did not match theirs.

You were approved of whether you were marginal or mainstream.

They provided a safe home to be in or come back to while launching you out of it when you were ready.

You knew they would help you fulfill your life goals by contributing, in whatever way they could, to your education and to your finding your unique path in the world.

They could let you go.

> How grateful I am for [my mother's] buoyant example, for the strong feeling of roots she gave me, for her conviction that, well-grounded, you can make the most of life, no matter what it brings.
> –Marion Rombauer Becker

From: *Triggers: How We Can Stop Reacting and Start Healing* (Shambhala)

Grief is our innate response to loss. When a memory of our childhood arises and we feel a pang of pain, anger, or regret, we have a program within us that can help us. We bring the memory to the three feelings in grief, sadness, anger, and fear:

We are *sad* about the love we missed out on or lost. This is how we work with our sense of loss.

We are *angry* at those who deprived us of love, made our lives a hell instead of the heaven love can make it. This is how we work with our sense of the unfairness of the loss.

We are *afraid* we might allow abuse in our present or future relationships or never get over what happened to us in childhood. This is how we work with our sense of threat or scarcity.

Now let's take a look at a five-step practice of grief-work:

1. We ask: "What was I *sad* about back then?" "What am I sad about now?" Then we let ourselves feel the sadness that goes with the memory.

   We ask: "What *anger* did I feel back then?" "What or whom am I angry at now?" We feel the anger.

   We ask: "What was I *scared* of back then?" "What am I afraid of now?" We feel the fear and assure ourselves that we don't have to act on it.

   We pause after each question and let the feeling or sensation have time to arise and last as long as it needs to. It will, with this permission from us over and over, on the heels of every memory, soon begin to fade and resolve itself.

2. We congratulate ourselves: "I am now taking care of myself as an adult. I am committed to growth and doing all I can to cultivate it."

3. We state the gratitude we feel for the grace to have found and become ready to tackle this practice.

4. Eventually, we might feel a shift. A grace happens in us and we begin letting go of ill-will, grudge, resentment, and the need to retaliate against our abusers. These four let-go's are the equivalent of forgiveness, something that happens in us not something we can cause at will.

5. We realize that our story and its emotions are identical to those of so many others all over the world who suffered as we did. We feel less isolated and victimized as we connect with them at a heart level. Now our compassion is for all who suffer everywhere, both victims and perpetrators. Look how grief has led us to loving-kindness!

From: *You Are Not What You Think: The Egoless Path to Self-Esteem and Generous Love* (Shambhala, 2015)

The Difference between Anger and Abuse

HEALTHY ANGER	AGGRESSION or ABUSE
Expresses a feeling in an authentic way	Becomes a tantrum in a theatrical way
Communicates, reports an impact	Puts down, bullies, or dumps on the other
Asks for a change in how we relate	Demands change or else threatens retribution
Is an I-Thou relationship, subject to subject	Feels like an I-It relationship, subject to object
Takes responsibility for the feeling	Blames and shames the other person
Is based on an intelligent assessment	Is based on judgment, making the other wrong
Sees the other as a *catalyst* for our feeling	Sees the other as the *cause* of our reaction
Is about an action or word that felt unfair	Is about indignation, a bruised ego
Focuses on the here and now	Is contaminated by similar past events
Is brief and let go of with a sense of closure (like a flare)	Is held on to as lingering resentment, hate, or grudge (like a smoldering fire)

HEALTHY ANGER	AGGRESSION or ABUSE
May be expressed with a red face, excited gestures, and a raised voice	May be expressed with a red face, menacing gestures, and a screaming voice
Says "Ouch!" assertively and respectfully while seeking a dialogue	Is aggressive and adversarial, is an attack based on ill-will and perhaps with an intent to harm
Informs the other	Intimidates, threatens the other
Is nonviolent, in control, and always shown within safe limits (manages temper)	Is violent, out of control, hostile, and punitive (loses temper)
Maintains good will at all times	Maintains a mean ill-will toward the other
Asks for accountability and amends to clear things up so forgiveness can happen	Seeks revenge, keeps holding something against the other, perhaps refusing repair of the relationship
Seeks mutual transformation	Seeks self-justification
Shows respect for the other as a peer	Shows contempt toward the other as a target
Aims at a deeper and more effective bond: an angry person moves *toward* the other	Wants to vent the rage no matter who gets hurt: an abuser moves *against* the other

HEALTHY ANGER	AGGRESSION or ABUSE
Acknowledges the element of grief	Feels grief but masks or denies it
Coexists with love, maintains connection	Cancels connection
Is fearless	Is fear-based
Is a form of addressing, processing, and resolving an issue with spiritual consciousness	*Is a form of avoiding one's own grief and distress about an issue with a refusal to work things out and thereby to grow spiritually*

When someone shows authentic anger, we feel safe so we stay put. We listen attentively and respond without defensiveness. "You are angry now and I will hear you out."

But when someone is abusive, our healthy response is to leave the premises since it is unsafe to stay put. When someone has crossed the line and is coming at us aggressively we say: "It is important to me to feel safe with you. So I will leave now and come back when you calm down. Then we can have a useful conversation."

From: *How To Be An Adult in Relationships* (Shambhala, 2022)

Letting Go of Ego-Centeredness

We or anyone might sometimes come across with an egotistical manner. This includes being arrogant, belligerent, entitled, controlling—the compulsions of a person driven by ego.

Here are some challenging practices that can help us let go of egotism and build a healthy ego, one with self-esteem, humility, and loving-kindness. The practices may seem over-the-top in what they ask of us, a radically spiritual way of living. Fortunately, we can all rely on grace from a higher power than ego to let that transformation happen in us.

1. Follow the Golden Rule: Act toward others as you would want them to act toward you.

2. Keep the needs of others in mind, especially in little ways—an antidote to selfishness.

3. Find some ways to maintain healthy self-esteem without showing off. It's OK to be a big shot; just don't act that way.

4. Let go of ranking, especially of elitism, seeing yourself as above others.

5. Acknowledge not knowing something or showing that you need support or help.

6. Take feedback as useful information rather than criticism, even when it is meant that way.

7. Apologize when you know you have harmed or offended anyone. Make amends if necessary.

8. Let go of attempts to control, dominate, or manipulate others.

9. Give people leeway and make allowances for their errors rather than pointing out, or picking them up on, every little thing they do that irks you.

10. Welcome disagreement because it can lead to dialogue. This puts the emphasis in a discussion on arriving at common ground or learning a new truth rather than proving yourself right.

11. Cooperate rather than compete; collaborate rather than have to show that you know best.

12. In a group, give up having to take center-stage. Trade in your own ego investment for the good of all the people concerned and for the accomplishment of the group goal.

13. Reconcile yourself to the given that you will not always get your way.

14. Don't hold a grudge against those who wrong you even when they won't admit it—and stop telling the story of how they offended you. Look for ways to reconcile rather than retaliate.

15. Remain on high alert for the entry of your reactive ego: the moment when you take what happened personally, become indignant, or interpret an action by someone as a slight to your dignity.

16. When someone's ego is aroused toward you, do not dig your heels in or go nose to nose. Simply pause with compassion toward the pain in his/her ego-reaction and treat it with loving-kindness, while, nonetheless, not putting up with any abuse.

17. In intimate bonds, give up vindicating yourself in order to gratify your ego and instead, let go of your ego to gratify the relationship. Become the protector of the partnership rather than the defender of your own ego.

18. Do good to those who hate you, pray for or wish enlightenment for those who have betrayed, failed, or mistreated you.

19. See losing face (and all these suggestions) as welcome opportunities for growth in humility, a virtue that makes you more lovable.

20. Discard the Ace (**A**rrogance-**C**ontrol-**E**ntitlement) of Ego for the Ace of Hearts.

Here are three ways of releasing ourselves from ego posturing:

> We notice our ego poses with a good-natured humor that finds something touching and amusing in them. Then we are less likely to keep using them.

> We use our ego-energy as a handy tool when appropriate, but without arrogance.

> We are thankful for the grace that helps us let go of ego-centeredness—even if it took the form of a hard-hitting comeuppance.

From: *You Are Not What You Think: The Egoless Path to Self-Esteem and Generous Love* (Shambhala)

When People Hate Us or Hurt our Feelings

A given of life is that people might hate us or hurt our feelings. Here is a summary glance at the three choices available to us when that happens.

A Primitive Reaction of Revenge from our Reptilian Brain:	A Commitment to "Do no harm" from our Ethical Sense:	An expression of Unconditional Loving-kindness from our Spiritual Consciousness:
We hurt or hate back.	We don't hurt or hate back.	We don't hurt or hate back. We go one step further and do good to those who hurt or hate us while our contact with them continues. Or we wish them the best, while choosing further contact.
We pay back.	We don't pay back.	We love back.
We act the way the other person has acted.	We act in a new and positive way.	We show unconditional love.

A Primitive Reaction of Revenge from our Reptilian Brain:	A Commitment to "Do no harm" from our Ethical Sense:	An expression of Unconditional Loving-kindness from our Spiritual Consciousness:
We obey an avenger's voice: "Do as you were done by."	We obey a mediator's voice: "Don't do as you were done by. Find a better way."	We hear Michelle Obama: "When they go low, we go high."
We become aggressive, actively or passively. We retaliate to "right the wrong" in accord with street-rule requirements.	We act in accord with moral principles and a commitment to nonviolence.	We act in accord with spiritual teachings such as the Sermon on the Mount or the Buddhist practice of loving-kindness or an extra big-hearted version of the Golden Rule.
An adrenaline/ testosterone-driven, face-saving reaction of ill will	An oxytocin/ heart-motivated sense of goodwill	An oxytocin-rich, open-hearted, sense of human solidarity

A Primitive Reaction of Revenge from our Reptilian Brain:	A Commitment to "Do no harm" from our Ethical Sense:	An expression of Unconditional Loving-kindness from our Spiritual Consciousness:
Ego-based, i.e., fear-based	Humanism-based	Love-based
"I alone am important!"	"You are important too!"	"We are deeply connected!"
We are giving in to our dark side.	We are showing our kind compassionate side.	We are opening to a grace that expands and deepens our commitment to love.
We are like the guys in the *Godfather* movies.	We are like Mr. Rogers or Atticus Finch.	We are Christ or Buddha in the world of today.
We enjoy the sense of power we feel by getting back at others and from looking good in the eyes of our gang.	We grow in self-respect because we are remaining true to our personal standards no matter how others act.	We love ourselves and all beings more and more. We are moving toward enlightenment/ transformation— and we want that for everyone.

A Primitive Reaction of Revenge from our Reptilian Brain:	A Commitment to "Do no harm" from our Ethical Sense:	An expression of Unconditional Loving-kindness from our Spiritual Consciousness:
Win-lose	Win-win	Oneness beyond winning or losing
Intimacy can't happen if we are in this column.	Intimacy can happen richly in this column.	Intimacy deepens and flourishes in this column.

Note that the far right column is counter-intuitive. We are acting from our evolved higher self not from our habit-impulse ego. We are awakened by grace in the form of a conversion from selfishness to selflessness, a surrendering of ego-centeredness to love-centeredness. That surrender is not a loss. It is a heart-opening. It is a response to our inborn impulse toward connection. That impulse shows us that in our deepest identity we are love. Thus, our loving-kindness toward all beings is a manifestation of who we really are.

From: *Triggers: How We Can Stop Reacting and Start Healing* (Shambhala)

How to Give Feedback Rather than Criticism

FEEDBACK:	CRITICISM:
Is the style of an assisting force	Is the style of an afflicting force
Informs us	Shames us
Is supportive	Is blaming / scolding / impugning / attacking
Is a reasonable assessment or correction	Is a judgment against us or a condemnation
Is meant to help, improve, or encourage us	Is meant to show us how wrong or inadequate we are
Is motivated by caring about our progress and growth	Is motivated by censure, blaming, and disapproval
Has our best interests at heart	Has reproach or rebuke in mind
Maintains an equal playing field, seeking "win-win"	May be competitive, playing the ego game of "Gotcha!"
Can be all positive or include well-meant critiquing: "constructive criticism" •	Is always negative

FEEDBACK:	CRITICISM:
Is about how we can both benefit: "Let's explore together."	Is about who is right and who is wrong: "I know and you don't."
Always values and contributes to bonding	Is willing to or does break connection
Seeks to open a dialogue and to learn from each another	Closes down communication, is dismissive
Is given privately or with others present if both are Ok with that	Might be private or might be in the presence of others, sometimes with the intent to embarrass us
Shows us by suggestion: a prompt	Tells us what is required: a poke
Feels trustworthy and inviting	Feels invasive or hurtful
Lifts us up	Puts us down
This is the style of an ally.	This is the style of a faultfinder.

A fun practice is to teach our inner critic how to switch to the kindly style of feedback!

From: *By Your Side: How to Find Soulful Allies and Become One to Others* (Shambhala, 2024)

The inner critic is a scolding voice in our head that hurls blame, shame, "can'ts" and "shoulds" at us. The inner critic is a mindset, usually from the past, a message we learned not one we were born with. It is an echo from people and institutions who judged or belittled us in the course of life. They include family, peers, religion, school, society. The inner critical voice is now internalized and feels like ourselves speaking.

Here are five ways to practice resetting our inner critical voice into one of self-advocacy. Choose any one or try one each day:

1. List three negative messages from your inner critic in your journal. Connect each statement to its origin, usually in early life. Was it appropriate then? Is it appropriate now? What shame did you feel? Where did you first hear this? Who said it? Were they trying to help or hurt you? Do this without blame of anyone only as an accessing of information.

2. Notice if the inner critic's vocabulary is absolute, "You always, you can't ever....." Under the absolute statement write a more inclusive one. Don't deny the main point only reduce it from absolute to relative: "Yes, I can't.." and "Sometimes I can...." Now you are changing a negative verdict against you into a neutral fact about all of us. You are reminding your inner critic, yourself, that inadequacy is a feature of being human. It is a given that all of us "sometimes" make mistakes, act inappropriately, fail. Let yourself

thereby feel a kinship with all other humans. Remind yourself that you also are committing yourself to do what you can to make up for your failings—all that really matters. Joe Biden said in 2020: "Failure at some point in life is inevitable but giving up is unforgivable."

3. Place the message of the inner critic into a mindfulness container: Sit with the statement and shear it of judgment, shame, belief, insult, triggering. Let it become only words in your head and label them as such. Do all this as you keep coming back to your breaths, lifelong teachers of taking in and letting go.

4. Call on the spiritual resource that fits for you. Ask for support in your practice:

> "Bodhisattvas, help me focus on your wisdom and compassion."

> "Holy Spirit, I thanks you for your gifts, help me appreciate them and put them to use."

> "May the universe join me in my personal evolution."

5. Here are three examples of combining the above practice with these spiritual resources:

1A. *Inner critic:* "You make stupid mistakes because you are stupid."

1B. *Your sane voice:* "Like all humans, I sometimes make mistakes. I also make up for them when I can."

1C. *Your higher self:* "I have received the gift of wisdom. May it keep opening in and through me. It is opening right now in this practice I am doing and being."

2A. *Inner critic:* "You will never amount to anything."

2B. *Your sane voice*: "Like all humans, I will sometimes be successful and sometimes not. I commit myself to do all I can to live a worthwhile life."

2.C *Your higher self:* "I am of great value to myself, others, and the world. May I deeply grasp this and be thankful for it."

3A. *Inner critic:* "You have nothing to offer a partner, or a career."

3B. *Your sane voice:* "Like all humans, I have some valuable qualities. I will keep gaining knowledge and skills. I have no control over whether someone will see them but I will keep showing them."

3C. *Your higher self:* "I have all the effulgent virtues and graces that any humans may have. I also keep upgrading my skillset to fulfill my calling. May I be thankful and keep sharing my gifts with the world around me."

From: *Ready: How to Know when to Go and when to Stay* (Shambhala)

Work with each of these commitments for whatever time it takes:

I AT MY BEST: MY PERSONAL STANDARDS

I am caring for my body by a healthy lifestyle. I am caring for my mind and spirit by psychological work on myself when needed and by faithfulness to spiritual practices too.

I am doing my best to keep my word, honor commitments, and follow through on the tasks I agree to do.

I am making every effort to abide by standards of rigorous honesty, equity, and respect for diversity in all my dealings no matter how others act toward me.

I forego taking advantage of others because of what I perceive as their lower status, or because of their weakness, neediness, misfortune, or their attachment to or idealizing of me. If I am in a position of power or authority I do not misuse it or become corrupted by it. My question is not "What can I get away with?" but "What is the right thing to do for all concerned?"

I keep examining my conscience with true candor. I am taking searching inventories not only about how I may have harmed others, but also about how I may not have activated my potentials or shared my gifts, how I may still be holding on to prejudices or the need to retaliate, how I may still not be as loving, inclusive, and open as I can be.

I now measure my success by how much steadfast love I have, not by how much I have in the bank, how much I achieve in business, how much status I have attained, or how much power I have over others. The central—and most exhilarating—focus of my life is to show my love in the style that is uniquely mine, in every way I can, here and now, always and everywhere, no one excluded.

I am letting go of the need to keep up appearances or to project a false or overly-impressive self-image. Now I want to appear as I am, without pretense and no matter how unflattering. The joy of transparency has become more important to me than making the "right" impression.

I appreciate positive feedback. I also welcome any well-intentioned critique that shows me where I might be less caring, less tolerant, less open than I can be. When I am shown up as a pretender or confronted about being mean or inauthentic, I am not defensive but take it as information about what I have to work on.

I am not trying to ingratiate myself with people in order to get on their good side. Being loved for who I am has become more important—and more interesting—than upholding or advancing the ever-shaky status of my ego.

I have come to accept that fear is a given of life, at least for me. But there is one thing I can commit myself to: I will not let fear *stop* me from doing what I need to do or *drive* me to do what I don't want to do.

I may meet or hear of someone who knows more than I, has more talent, or is more successful. I am letting go of envy and rivalry. Now I find myself admiring that person and trying to learn from him or her. I am accepting the given that we all have different gifts in different quantities. As I move from the envy that divides to the admiration that connects I feel a kinship with all my fellow humans, a joy indeed. I also notice that I can love myself and that I become more lovable too.

As I say yes to the reality of who I am, with pride in my gifts and unembarrassed awareness of my limits, I find myself living in accord with my own deepest needs, values, and wishes, not those of others.

I appreciate that whatever love or wisdom I may have or show comes not *from* me but *through* me. I give thanks for these encouraging graces and say yes to the stirring call to live up to them.

I WITH OTHERS: THE GUIDELINES I HONOR

I appreciate the ways others love me, no matter how limited. I am letting go of expecting—or demanding—that they love me exactly as I want them to. I am letting go of wanting others to prove that they love me. At the same time, I can always ask for the kind of love I long for.

I am learning to trust others when the record shows they can be trusted while I, nonetheless, commit myself to being trustworthy regardless of what others may do.

I remain open to reconciling with others after conflict. At the same time, I am learning to release—with love and without blame—those who show themselves to be unwilling to relate to me respectfully.

I accept, without judgment, the given of sudden unexplained absence, ghosting, or the silent treatment by others and will not use those styles myself.

I do not allow the judgments or impressions of others to contaminate my personal relationships. As a mindfulness practice, I am relating to people in my life based on my own experience, not on tales I hear about them. I ask the same of those close to me: "You are who you are to me because of how I experience you and I ask that I be who I am to you because of how you experience me."

When a family member suddenly cuts off communication with me, I ask for dialogue so we can repair the rupture. If the family member refuses I respect that choice while remaining available for communication to resume. On my part, I choose not to ostracize family members who have offended me. Nor do I join other family members in their boycott against someone. When I meet up with family rejection, I grieve the situation and stay open to reconciliation.

I am learning to be assertive by asking for what I need or want. I ask without demand, expectation, manipulation, or a sense of entitlement. I show respect for the timing and choices of others by being able to take no for an answer.

I respect the freedom of others, especially those I love. I do not want to use any charms of body, word, or mind to trick or deceive anyone. I want others to have what they want. I am not trying to manipulate or intimidate others into doing what I want them to do.

I do not knowingly hurt or intend to offend others. I act kindly toward others not to impress them, win their approval, or obligate them but because I really am kind—or working on it. If others fail to thank me or to return my kindness, that does not have to stop me from behaving lovingly nonetheless. When I fail at this—or at any of these commitments—I can admit it, make amends, and resolve to act differently next time. Now I can say "Oops!" and apologize more easily and willingly when necessary.

If people occasionally hurt me, I can say "Ouch" --in lower case letters or in all caps! I can ask to open a dialogue. I may ask for amends but I can drop the topic if they are not forthcoming. No matter what, I do not choose to get even, hold grudges, keep a record of wrongs, or hate anyone. "What goes around comes around" has become "May what goes around come around in a way that helps everyone learn and grow." I am thereby hoping for the transformation of others rather than retribution against them. I am seeking repair not revenge.

I am noticing that my capacity to forgive others—and myself—is expanding all the time. My forgiveness of others is a letting go of blame, ill will, and the need for revenge. This transformation by grace feels like a true liberation from ego.

I do not let others abuse me and, internally, I want to interpret their harshness as coming from their own pain and as a sadly confused way of letting me know they need connection but don't know how to ask for it in healthy ways. I recognize this with concern and compassion not with censure or scorn.

I do not gloat over the sufferings or defeats of those who have hurt me or those whom I dislike. "It serves them right!" has changed to: "May this serve to help them evolve."

I realize that I, like all humans, have repressed and disavowed some negative and positive parts of myself. I am finding ways to uncover this shadow side of myself: My strong dislike of certain *negative* traits in others makes me ask if I have similar traits in myself. My strong admiration for the *positive* qualities in others reminds me to look for the same gifts in myself.

I have a sense of humor but not at the expense of others. I want to use humor to poke fun at human foibles, especially my own. I do not tell racist or biased jokes nor do I listen to them. I do not engage in ridicule, mocking, put-downs, snide, derogatory, demeaning, or bigoted remarks, sarcasm or "comebacks." When others use hurtful humor toward me I want to feel the pain in both of us and look for ways to bring more mutual respect into our communication.

I do not hold anyone in contempt. I do not laugh at people for their mistakes and misfortunes but I am looking for ways to be understanding and supportive.

I do not try to embarrass people by shaming or making them look bad in front of other people.

No matter how busy or in a hurry I am I choose to act with patience and attentiveness toward others rather than to be curt, abrupt, or dismissive.

I am practicing ways to express my anger against unfairness directly and nonviolently rather than in abusive, bullying, threatening, blaming, out-of-control, vengeful, or passive ways.

I am less and less concerned with being right or on insisting that I be acknowledged as the one who is right. I am letting go of any demand that others agree with me. I am now more apt to listen to and appreciate the contributions of others, while also sharing my own view in a collaborative dialogue. I do this without trying to defend myself or promote my view. I want having to be right to be transformed into hearing rightly, speaking rightly, and acting rightly.

I notice how there are people who are sometimes excluded from the in-group. Rather than be comforted that I am still safely an insider, especially by joining in gossiping about them, I want to sense the pain in being an outsider. Then I can reach out and be sure to include everyone in my circle of love, compassion, and respect.

In a group situation, when someone is shamed, humiliated, or harshly criticized, I do not want to be glad that the finger was not pointed at me. I want to support the victim of aggression by asking for a respectful tone in the dialogue. I know that standing up for the victim may turn the bully's fury on me so I am continually working on building up my courage.

I want to be loyal to any association of which I am a member. At the same time, I know that my affiliation does not preclude becoming a whistle-blower if necessary. I remain faithful to the organization but not to a cover-up. I also know I have to take my leave if it no longer abides by its mission.

I look at other people and their choices with intelligent discernment but without judgment or censure. I still notice the shortcomings of others and myself, but now I am beginning to see them as facts to deal with rather than flaws to be criticized or be ashamed of. Accepting others as they are has become more important than whether they are what I want them to be.

I avoid criticizing, interfering, or giving advice that is not specifically asked for. I take care of myself by staying away from those who use this intrusive approach toward me, while still holding them in my spiritual circle of loving-kindness.

I am willing to participate in the harmless conventions and social rituals that make others happy, for example, family dinners or acknowledgment of birthdays. If a social or family situation begins to become toxic, I excuse myself politely.

I am less and less competitive in relationships at home and work and find happiness in cooperation and community. I shun situations in which my winning means that others lose in a humiliating way.

I never give up on believing that everyone has an innate goodness and that being loved by me can contribute to bringing it out.

In intimate bonds, I honor equality, keep agreements, work on problems, and act in loving and trustworthy ways. My goal is not to use a relationship to gratify my ego but to dispossess myself of ego to gratify the relationship.

My partner—or prospective partner—and I can contemplate this list together. These commitments can become the ground rules of our relationship. With this as a pre-nuptial agreement we have found the path to trusting one another.

I want my sexual style to adhere to the same standards of integrity and loving-kindness that apply in all areas of my life. More and more, my sexuality expresses love, passion, and joyful playfulness. I also remain committed to a responsible adult style of relating and enjoying.

I IN THE WORLD: MY EMBRACING REACH

I feel a caring concern for the world around me. I look for ways to work for justice and commit myself to nonviolence. I support restorative rather than retributive justice. I feel myself called to action by violations of human rights, prejudice, hate crimes, gun violence, genocide, nuclear armaments, economic injustice, climate change, ecological exploitation. I remain respectful of diversity and dedicated to equity. I keep educating myself on all these issues.

Confronted with the suffering in the world, I do not turn my eyes away, nor do I get stuck in blaming God or humanity but simply ask: "What then shall *I* do? What is the opportunity in this for my practice of loving-kindness?" I keep finding ways to respond even if they have to be minimal: "It is better to light one candle than to curse the darkness."

With planetary consciousness, I tread with care on the earth with what St. Bonaventure called "a courtesy toward natural things."

These ideals are becoming my personal standards. I trust them as pathways to psychological and spiritual maturity. I already notice how they are boosting my self-esteem. I like myself more when I follow ideals like these. And I know I am on the trail of becoming a true human being.

I notice that each entry on this list offers me an *empowerment.* I feel myself stronger, more self-assured, more at home in the world, more able to handle whatever comes my way—and everything seems lighter too: "Month by month, things are losing their hardness; even my body now lets the light through." (Virginia Woolf: *The Waves*)

I am not hard on myself when I fail to live up to these ideals. I just keep practicing earnestly. The sincerity of my intention and my dedication to ongoing effort feel like the equivalent of success. I can feel myself letting go of perfectionism and of guilt about not being perfect.

I do not seek praise or recognition for how I may honor this list. Nor do I demand or expect that others follow it.

I am sharing this list with those who are open to it.

I keep placing the intention—or praying—that someday these commitments can become the style not only of individuals but of groups in the world community: corporate, political, religious.

Now I see my own participation in work, politics, or religion as part of my spiritual commitment to co-create a world of justice, peace, and love.

> May I show all the love I have
> In any way I can
> Today and all the time,
> To everyone—including me—
> Since love is what we really are
> And what we're here to show.
> Now nothing matters to me more
> Or gives me greater joy.
> May all our world become
> One Sacred Heart of love.

From: *Wholeness and Holiness: How to Be Sane, Spiritual, and Saintly* (Orbis Books)

Our Concentric Circles of Loving-kindness
Beginning with Ourselves
and Extending into the Entire World

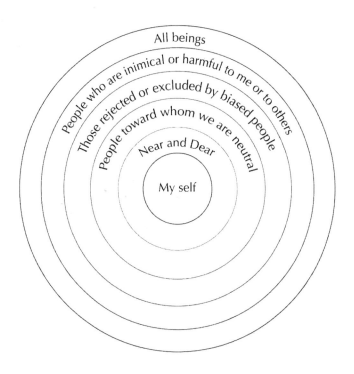

I say Yes to everything that happens to me today
as an opportunity
to give or receive love and to free myself from fear.

I am thankful for the enduring capacity to love
that has come to me
from the Sacred Heart
of the universe.

May everything that happens to me today
open my heart more and more.

May all that I think, say, feel, do, and am
express loving-kindness
toward myself, those close to me, and all beings.

May love be my life purpose, my bliss,
my destiny, my calling,
the richest grace I can receive or give.

And may I always be especially compassionate
toward people who are considered least or last
or who feel alone or lost.

From: *The Power Of Grace: Recognizing Unexpected Gifts on the Path* (Shambhala)

No matter how we were treated in our past, no matter what is happening to us now, no matter what may come our way in future days, our capacity to love can never go away or even wane. Love is the diamond essence that is our true self, ineradicable, unending, indissoluble. This innermost core, at the heart of our being, love, holds us and at the same time hurls us into the waiting world. Love wants only to beam in, from, and through us every day, everywhere, to everyone. Love wants to happen. All we have to do is not get in its way:

As I face things as they are, without self-deception or wishful thinking, my predicament discloses a path.

I begin to see my next step and notice I have the courage to take it.

I let go of expectations; I acknowledge reality: "I went in with no expectations and they were all met."

I am choosing to have no escape hatch.

I am not trying to fix or control the situation I find myself in.

As I let the chips fall where they may, I find ways to make the best of how they land.

My Yes to what is, and to how I and others are, has become unconditional.

I notice that as I accept how others are and how I am, I no longer judge myself or others. Opening to my yes of welcome cancels my no of rejecting.

Now I see that everything that happens to me is somehow a grace, a gift from the sacred heart of the universe, a light that will not go out, something enfolding me and unfolding in me.

I trust that I have inner resources to see me through this and any predicament.

May all people find this path to healing and hope.

Since everything that happens to or in me, without exception, offers an opportunity for progress on the spiritual path, reality itself is holy.

Every time I face life as it is, rather than deny, avoid, or oppose it, I am in touch with the divine in me and all around.

From: *Ready: How to Know when to Go and When to Stay* (Shambhala, 2022)

Even after all the dark events of recent history, I still believe we can trust that, deep-down, we are a most pure goodness, consciousness, and bliss. We do not have to search for all this light, only commit ourselves to integrity and loving-kindness and it will beam through us and through everything that happens to us. Then, with unwearying tenderness, we can share it with all our fellow pilgrims. No, it does not take long to notice the good news that light is our true nature and that love is how we show it.

From: *Everyday Commitments* (Shambhala, 2008)

What makes us human beings so uniquely wonderful in this puzzling universe is that we never give up on love. Against all odds, with no guarantee of being loved in return, out of the hate and hurt so often handed us, in the face of the sad suffering history has let us see, we go on loving. What deep respect we deserve for this capacity of ours to make love out of anything and to let it last.

From: *How to be an Adult* (Paulist Press, 1991)

Since everything that happens to us,
without exception,
offers us an opportunity for grace,
reality itself is holy.
So every time we face reality,
rather than deny or oppose it,
we are being deeply spiritual.

From: *When Mary Becomes Cosmic: A Jungian and Mystical Path to the Divine Feminine*
(Paulist Press, 2016)

What have we ever,
More or better,
Than our life together?

From: *By Your Side* (Shambhala, 2024)

David Richo, Ph.D., is psychotherapist, writer, and workshop leader. He shares his time between Santa Barbara and San Francisco, California. Dave combines psychological and spiritual perspectives in his work. His website is davericho.com

Books:

How to Be An Adult: A Handbook on Psychological and Spiritual Integration (Paulist Press, 1991)

When Love Meets Fear: How to Become Defense-less and Resource-full (Paulist Press, 1997)

Shadow Dance: Liberating the Power and Creativity of Your Dark Side (Shambhala, 1999)

How To Be An Adult in Relationships: The Five Keys to Mindful Loving (Shambhala, 2002)
(Revised Edition, 2021)

The Five Things We Cannot Change and the Happiness We Find by Embracing Them (Shambhala, 2005)

The Power of Coincidence: How Life Shows Us What We Need to Know (Shambhala, 2007)

The Sacred Heart of the World: Restoring Mystical Devotion to Our Spiritual Life (Paulist Press, 2007)

Everyday Commitments: Choosing a Life of Love, Realism, and Acceptance (Shambhala, 2007)

When the Past Is Present: Healing the Emotional Wounds That Sabotage Our Relationships (Shambhala, 2008)

Being True to Life: Poetic Paths to Personal Growth (Shambhala, 2009)

Daring to Trust: Opening Ourselves to Real Love and Intimacy (Shambhala, 2010)

Coming Home to Who You Are: Discovering Your Natural Capacity for Love, Integrity, and Compassion (Shambhala, 2011)

How to Be an Adult in Faith and Spirituality (Paulist Press, 2011)

How To Be An Adult in Love: Letting Love in Safely and Showing it Recklessly (Shambhala, 2013)

The Power of Grace: Recognizing Unexpected Gifts on the Path (Shambhala, 2014)

When Catholic Means Cosmic: Opening to a Big-Hearted Faith (Paulist Press, 2015)

You Are Not What You Think: The Egoless Path to Self-Esteem and Generous Love (Shambhala, 2015)

When Mary Becomes Cosmic: A Jungian and Mystical Path to the Divine Feminine (Paulist Press, 2016)

The Five Longings: What We've Always Wanted and Already Have (Shambhala, 2017)

Everything Ablaze: Meditating on the Mystical Vision of Teilhard de Chardin   (Paulist Press, 2017)

Five True Things: A Little Guide to Embracing Life's Big Challenges   (Shambhala, 2019)

Triggers: How We Can Stop Reacting and Start Healing   (Shambhala, 2019)

Wholeness and Holiness: How to Be Sane, Spiritual, and Saintly   (Orbis Books, 2020)

Ready: How to Know when to Go and when to Stay (Shambhala, 2022)

To Thine Own Self Be True: Shakespeare as Therapist and Spiritual Guide   (Paulist Press, 2023)

By Your Side: How to Find Soulful Allies and Become an Ally to Others   (Shambhala, 2024)

You are welcome to copy and share any pages from this book. Please include the book reference and website: davericho.com.

Made in the USA
Middletown, DE
30 December 2024

68465654R00040